The Essential Mary Poppins

101 Things You Didn't Know About the Timeless Film and Legendary Cast

by
Horace Martin Woodhouse
Author, *The Essential Wizard of Oz*

COPYRIGHT NOTICE

The Essential Mary Poppins: 101 Things You Didn't Know About the Timeless Film and Legendary Cast is published and copyrighted © 2014 by History Company LLC (www.historycompany.com). All rights reserved. No part of this book may be reproduced in any form by any electronic or mechanical means (including photocopying, recording, or information storage or retrieval) without permission in writing from the publisher. Users are not permitted to mount any part of this book on the World Wide Web. Requests to the publisher for permission should be addressed to the Permissions Department: support@historycompany.com

Limit of Liability/Disclaimer of Warranty: While the publisher and the author have used their best efforts in preparing this book, they make no representations or warranties with respect to the accuracy or completeness of the contents of this book. No warranty may be created or extended by sales representatives or written sales materials. Neither the publisher nor the author shall be liable for any loss of profit or any other commercial damages, including but not limited to special, incidental, consequential, or other damages resulting from the use of the information contained herein.

History Company books are available at special discounts for bulk purchases of 12 units or more (shipping and handling charges apply). For more information, contact:

History Company, LLC
373 Enfield Falls Road, Ithaca, NY 14850
(800) 891-0466

Printed in the United States of America.

"Once in a lifetime – and only once – a picture comes along which cannot be compared to any other and to which no other can be compared. A picture which writes a new page in motion picture history... You have made it – Mary Poppins."

– Sam Goldwyn (in a letter to Walt Disney)

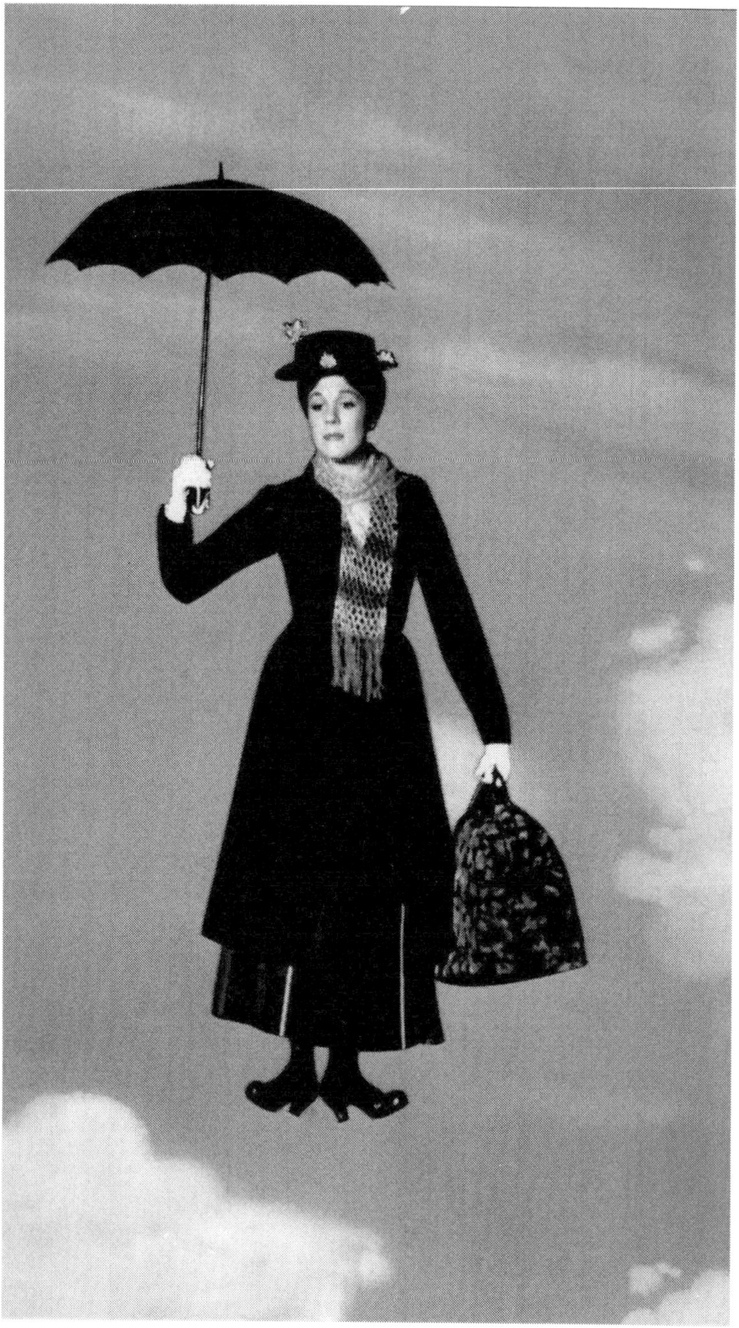

Practically Perfect in Every Way

Although the story of a magically empowered English nanny was originally told in a series of books by P. L. Travers, most of the world knows Mary Poppins as the central character in the film created by Walt Disney. A cinematic confection, *Mary Poppins* has enraptured generations of moviegoers since its premiere fifty years ago, standing with *The Wizard of Oz* as the two greatest children's films adapted from books.

Hollis Alpert, writing in the *Saturday Review*, called it "one of the most magnificent pieces of entertainment ever to come from Hollywood." A masterpiece by any standard, *Mary Poppins* is a triumph of imagination and ingenuity, one of Disney's major contributions to American cinema.

Given its ubiquity in popular culture and its place in the hearts of moviegoers of all ages, one wonders, after all this time, if there could be anything more we don't already know about it. But no matter how familiar the characters, how memorable the music, how timeless the story, the answer is, yes, there's a whole book worth of things most of us will be surprised to learn. You're holding that book in your hands.

The Essential Mary Poppins is brimming with amazing true stories, corrected myths, and particular particulars about one of the most remarkable movie musicals of all time. It's not meant to provide a comprehensive nor complete academic reference, but rather an accessible distillation, served in small bites (each like a spoonful of sugar), about a film that has resonated across half a century.

Browse through this little book to satisfy your curiosity. It's guaranteed to reveal things you never knew about *Mary Poppins*.

— Horace Martin Woodhouse

By the mid-1930s, Walter Elias "Walt" Disney had established himself as an accomplished Hollywood animated-short producer. Then, on December 21, 1937, his first feature-length film, *Snow White and the Seven Dwarfs*, opened to the public in Los Angeles. The audience laughed at Dopey's antics, cried at the death sleep of Snow White, and gave the film a standing ovation at the end. The success of *Snow White* allowed Walt to build a new studio.

The following year, Walt picked up a book on the bedside table of his daughter Diane Marie, and as he read about the English nanny who could fly, he recognized the potential for a film adaptation. In the years that followed, he tried and failed to gain rights to transfer the beloved story to film, as the book's author, P. L. Travers, rejected his advances. She didn't believe a film version would do justice to her creation.

Born Helen Lyndon Goff in Australia in 1899, Pamela Lyndon Travers began writing her series of children's stories about the magical nanny named Mary Poppins in 1933. She used only her initials, hiding her gender to avoid being dismissed as an archetypal female author of children's books. Travers explained that the name "M. Poppins" originated from childhood stories she contrived for her sisters (with mannerisms and attitude of her central character likely inspired by her stern but warm-hearted great aunt, Helen Morehead).

A master of persistence, Walt Disney had lusted after the *Poppins* stories for nearly twenty years before Pamela Travers succumbed to "such a generous contract that it would not be right to refuse any longer," and despite, in her words to a friend, her belief that "Disney was completely without subtlety and emasculated any creature he touched, replacing truth with false sentimentality." In 1961, Travers' lawyer, Lord Goodman, of Goodman Derrick, London, negotiated payment of five percent of the movie gross, with a guarantee of $100,000 ($750,00 in 2014 dollars), and script approval – unprecedented concessions at the time. However, Disney retained final draft approval and final say on the finished print of the film.

The agreement began what Travers called an "uneasy wedlock," and her objections continued all through the production. She fruitlessly attempted to protect her creation from being corrupted by the forces of pop culture – the Mary Poppins she imagined was a very different woman from the Walt Disney nanny. Her objections were listened to and at times changes were made. There were other times and other issues and demands where Disney overruled her, citing contract stipulations that he had final say on the finished print.

When Travers met with the Sherman brothers to hear the songs they had written for the film, her opening line was, "I don't even know why I'm meeting you gentlemen, because in fact we're not going to have music in this film and, in fact, we're not going to have any prancing and dancing."

Sons of Tin Pan Alley songwriter Al Sherman ("You Gotta Be a Football Hero"), the team of Robert and Richard Sherman had their first Top Ten hit with "Tall Paul," recorded by Disney Mouseketeer Annette Funicello. The success of their song brought the brothers to the attention of Walt Disney, who eventually hired them on as staff songwriters for the Disney Studios. Walt assigned the Shermans to write songs for *Mary Poppins*, even before he had secured film rights from Pamela Travers. The brothers wrote over thirty numbers, fourteen of which made it to the final cut.

Bill Walsh joined Walt Disney Studios in 1943, working for both the Publicity and Story departments. One of his jobs was scripting the Mickey Mouse daily comic strip (drawn by Floyd Gottfredson), which he continued doing for more than 20 years. Walt Disney, who used television to promote his theatrical films, chose Walsh to head the studio's television division, and after several seasons on *The Mickey Mouse Club*, Walsh left to produce live-action films. For his work on *Mary Poppins*, Walsh shared Academy Award nominations for Best Picture with Walt Disney, and also for Best Writing (Based on Material from Another Medium), an award he shared with Don DaGradi.

It was Don DaGradi's skill as an artist and his love of visual gags – people floating through the air and flying up the chimney – that enhanced the fun and fantasy of the film.

Travers wanted the cast to be entirely English, in keeping with her books. However, Walsh and DaGradi set out to assemble a blend of English and American actors for wider commercial appeal, and Disney wanted a big name to play Mary Poppins. Stage actress Mary Martin was the first choice, but she decided against a return to film. Bette Davis was considered, but as the score developed, it appeared that the role would require a singing actress. Disney began thinking that Mary Poppins could be played by a younger actress when Robert Sherman came to him with a suggestion. He had just seen Julie Andrews on *The Ed Sullivan Show* (March 19, 1961), performing songs from *Camelot*, the musical she was appearing in on Broadway. Sherman was the first person to imagine twenty-seven-year-old Julie Andrews as Mary Poppins, particularly impressed with her pitch-perfect whistling during "What Do the Simple Folk Do," a duet with Richard Burton.

Her vocal range spanned four octaves, while most people are only capable of three. Born Julia Elizabeth Wells, Julie Andrews became a professional at age 12, and she appeared on the bill at a royal command performance a year later. By 15, she was the family's breadwinner, and at two days shy of her 19th birthday, she made her debut on Broadway, where she would go on to triumph as Eliza Doolittle in *My Fair Lady*. Her role as Mary Poppins would cement her stardom.

Disney followed-up on Sherman's suggestion and arranged for a trip to New York City to catch a matinee performance of *Camelot*. After the show, convinced that she would be the best actress for the part, he introduced himself to Andrews in her dressing room and asked if she might be interested in playing the role of Mary Poppins – he was sure enough about her performance to make an immediate offer. Disney enthusiastically described the film project, and invited Andrews and her husband, costume designer Tony Walton, out to Hollywood to hear the songs and see the designs that had been created. He took the couple on a personal tour of his studios and to Disneyland. To further entice Andrews, he suggested hiring Walton as costume designer and visual consultant.

Tony Walton began his career as costume designer with the Broadway production of Noel Coward's *Conversation Piece* in 1957. He alternated between designing for the London and New York stages throughout the late 1950s and early 60s, and entered films as costume designer and visual consultant for *Mary Poppins* which starred his then-wife Julie Andrews.

Pamela Travers not only objected to the altering of Mary Poppins' character from cold and intimidating in the novel to warm and cheery in the film, she actually protested the use of the color red in the film. Yet Walton chose a spun-sugar palate of color for his costumes and even managed to add a touch of red – his signature color – to Mary's otherwise prim costumes. For Bert's jacket in the "Jolly Holiday" sequence, he had different widths of ribbon sewn onto a white jacket. The eye-popping costumes (made by Elizabeth Courtney) earned Walton the first of five Oscar nominations.

Julie Andrews was not certain she wanted to make her screen debut as a flying nanny. She only agreed to make *Mary Poppin*s after being passed over for the role of Eliza Doolittle in the film adaptation of *My Fair Lady*. Andrews had won critical acclaim after originating the character on Broadway, but was shockingly dropped in favor of Audrey Hepburn for the Hollywood adaptation. It remains the biggest casting controversy in motion picture history.

Walt became obsessed with *Mary Poppins* the way he hadn't been since the early days of the studio. He worked day and night for months, even moving his office into the studio. Throughout filming, Walt kept "plussing" the picture: The nannies don't simply walk away from the Banks' home at the beginning of the film, they are whisked away by the wind. The chimney sweeps' dance on the rooftops of London doesn't just end with a bow. Walt added fireworks to the finish.

Travers' biggest objection to the film was the way Disney portrayed the central character. The Disney version of Mary Poppins had to become less vain, nasty, cold and intimidating than the book character and this was difficult for Travers to swallow. She thought that Julie Andrews was all wrong for the lead, much too pretty to play Mary.

The illustrations in the books show the nanny with a turned up nose, her appearance based on a wooden peg Dutch doll that Travers loved as a young girl. At their first meeting, Travers took one look at Andrews and remarked, "You've got the nose for it," referring to her *retroussé* nose, and reluctantly warmed to idea of Andrews as Mary.

Andrews was a smoker at the time, so, according to Karen Dotrice, the actress who played young Jane Banks, during breaks "there'd be Mary Poppins with a cigarette hanging out of her mouth!" (Interesting to note that Walt Disney was a well-known chain smoker).

The character of Bert, a vagabond with various odd jobs, including a one-man band street performer, a sidewalk artist, and a chimney sweep, is an amalgamation of several characters from the books. Walt had originally considered offering the role to Anthony Newley, Danny Kaye, Fred Astaire, or Tommy Steele, among others. Dick Van Dyke was starring in his own sitcom at the time, in the role of TV comedy writer Rob Petrie on *The Dick Van Dyke Show*, but when he was suggested for Bert, Walt admitted he had never seen him on television. After viewing a segment of the show in a projection room, he decided immediately to cast Van Dyke in the role.

It was Dick Van Dyke's casting that Travers opposed most. She suggested the male lead was better suited to a British actor like Laurence Olivier or Richard Burton.

To prepare for playing his character, Dick Van Dyke worked on developing a typical Cockney (or working-class English slang) dialect with British character actor J. Pat O'Malley. The result was a version of Cockney speech that has been named one of the worst accent attempts in film history. O'Malley, it seems, did not speak with a Cockney dialect. Although he was born in England, his ancestry was Irish. It was the case of an Irishman trying to teach an American to speak Cockney.

O'Malley is an uncredited voice as the Cockney coster in the "Supercalifragilisticexpialidocious" sequence as well as the master of hounds, a hound, a horse, a photographer, a reporter and the pearlie drummer. In other work for Disney he provided voices for Jasper, the bumbling henchman, in *101 Dalmatians* and Colonel Hathi, the Indian elephant, in *The Jungle Book*.

Plenty of criticism has been levelled at Dick Van Dyke's Cockney accent over the years, but the actor has never heard a bad word aimed at his loose-limbed dancing in *Mary Poppins*, despite the fact that he was never trained as a dancer and did not begin dancing until he was in his thirties. As a struggling alcoholic he would go to work with terrible hangovers, which he admitted, "if you're dancing is really hard." (Van Dyke overcame alcoholism in the 1970s).

Although Dick Van Dyke considers *Mary Poppins* the best film of his career, he nevertheless maintains to this day that he was somewhat miscast as Bert. He has suggested that either Jim Dale or Ron Moody would have been better in the part.

Walt was totally involved in every aspect of the film. Although the book was written in the mid-30s, he moved the time of the movie back to the turn of the century, as a more colorful time period for the story. With an intimate knowledge of London, he was fascinated by the buskers who made a living by entertaining in pubs and on the city's streets. He introduced the idea of having Bert make music as a one-man band. He remembered the chalk artists who drew scenes on the sidewalk in front of the National gallery, so the script included Bert's sidewalk mural. He also suggested a fantasy sequence in which horses leaped off a carousel and raced through the countryside.

In the early stages of production, Van Dyke was being tested in various makeups for later sequences. To relieve the boredom, he entertained crew members with comic routines, among them the "stepping down" routine of an old man trying his best to step off a curb without tipping over. When Walt viewed the test in a projection room, he not only decided to cast Van Dyke as Mr. Dawes, the elderly director of the bank where Mr. Banks works, he specifically requested that crew members "build a six-inch riser on the board room set so Dick can do that stepping-down routine."

During the film's end titles, "Navckid Keyd" is credited as Mr. Dawes Sr, an anagram of "Dick Van Dyke."

The first scenes filmed were for the "Jolly Holiday" sequence so that animators could begin work early in the project. Milt Kahl, often considered the finest draughtsman of the Disney animators, created most of the characters in the animated sequence. (Kahl became Walt Disney's "nephew" when he married Phyllis Bounds, Lillian Disney's niece).

For the "Jolly Holiday" song, the Sherman brothers suggested that one of the choruses should be sung by waiters harmonizing as a barbershop quartet. Walt said that waiters had always reminded him of penguins and proposed using animated penguins for the sequence. (Animator Frank Thomas discovered there are 26 varieties of penguins, so he drew the look most people think of as a penguin).

When Van Dyke landed the role of Bert, he was asked by Walt to recommend a choreographer. Van Dyke came up with the team of Marc Breaux and Dee Dee Wood, husband and wife who worked with him on *The Jack Benny Show*. Breaux and Wood were two of only three major members of the production staff who had not worked previously for Disney; the third was musical arranger Irwin Kostal.

Breaux and Wood created the dance for the penguins (animals who have neither shoulders, a bendable waist, or knees). Wood was filmed performing the dance as a study guide for the animators, and they used life-sized cut outs of penguins to show Dick Van Dyke where to look during the routine.

Frank Thomas and Ollie Johnston (two of Disney's core of animators called the "Nine Old Men") animated the penguin dance and famously complained that Dick Van Dyke kept stepping on their penguins while they were figuring out where to place the characters.

The expansion of Bert's role would cause one of Travers' major concerns about the Disney script. She demanded that any suggestions of romance between Mary and Bert be eliminated, so lyrics for "Jolly Holiday" seem to indicate that their friendship is purely platonic. (Some subtle hints of romance, however, remain in the finished film.) Once asked whether she thinks Mary and Bert ever got together, Julie Andrews said, "I hope so. She wouldn't admit it, but I do hope so."

Van Dyke as Bert explains, "Good luck will rub off when I shakes hands with you," reflecting a real belief in Britain during the era, that chimney sweeps were "lucky" and able to make other people "lucky."

"Chim-Chim-Cheree" was inspired by an animator's sketch of a chimney sweep carrying his brooms and whistling, and the Sherman brothers originally planned to use the song for the chimney sweeps' dance atop the London rooftops. But that changed after Peter Ellenshaw, the British-born matte artist and designer, described a ritual from his college days in which young men, after a pint or two at the local pub, would lock arms and dance to the tune of "Knees Up, Mother Brown" while raising their knees as high as possible. The Shermans adapted the old song to produce "Step in Time."

For the "Step in Time" sequence, choreographers Breaux and Wood had art director William Tuntke make a model of the rooftop set so they could stage rehearsals with the dancers. They rehearsed for six weeks, then spent another full week to get it on film.

One of Julie Andrews' favorite songs written for the score was the lullaby, "Stay Awake." When she heard there might be plans to delete it, she wrote a letter of concern to Pamela Travers who insisted that the song remain in the film. Andrews struggled through nearly fifty takes in the Disney recording studio before she was happy with how it sounded.

In contrast, it too Dick Van Dyke only one take to record his verses as Mr. Dawes for "Fidelity, Fiduciary Bank." He got it right the first time.

The word was never used in the original books. According to Richard Sherman, it took him and his brother several weeks to come up with the word "Supercalifragilisticexpialidocious," based on doubletalk from their childhood at summer camp in the Adirondacks, the scene of a contest for who could invent a longer word than "antidisestablishmentarianism."

A copyright infringement lawsuit was brought by Barney Young and Gloria Parker, who had written a song in 1949 entitled "Supercalafajaistickespeealadojus," seeking twelve million dollars in damages. They lost because Disney lawyers were able to present evidence showing that the nonsense word had been around, in some form or another, for decades.

The word was added to the *Oxford English Dictionary* in 1986.

The song, "Let's Go Fly a Kite" was inspired by the Sherman brothers' own father, Al Sherman, who made his own kites and took the boys to fly them at Roxbury Park in Beverly Hills.

It's the film's feel-good finale, as the cold-hearted Mr. Banks mends the kite and celebrates his realization that spending time with his children is more important than his job. The song took an idiom that is so often used negatively – "go fly a kite!" – and turned it into a positive proclamation.

Walt had no training in music, but he had an instinctive understanding of what he wanted in the movie's songs. He shook his head when the Sherman boys first performed "Supercalifragilisticexpialidocious." "Something is wrong there," he said. "Why don't you try speeding it up a little bit?"

The song, "Let's Go Fly a Kite" was originally written in 4/4 or common time, but Walt felt it was too much like the ending of a Broadway show and wanted a song that was more "breezy," like a waltz. The song was re-crafted into a 3/4 waltz-like arrangement.

The concept for "A Spoonful of Sugar" in the sequence where Mary and the children clean up the nursery came about when Robert Sherman's son received polio vaccine at school that was injected into a cube of sugar instead of administered as a shot. The vaccine was not the Salk vaccine, which was injected, but the Sabin vaccine, which was served to millions of schoolchildren in a spoon with a cube of sugar. Robert suggested to his brother that the song be called "a spoonful of sugar helps the medicine go down." Richard put the phrase to music and the song was born.

The robin that lands on Mary's finger in the "Spoonful of Sugar" sequence is an American Robin (*Turdus migratorius*), not a European Robin (*Erithacus rubecula*), common in the United Kingdom.

Director Robert Stevenson originally hired a professional bird whistler for "A Spoonful of Sugar," but it sounded "too smooth," so Julie offered to do it herself.

In the "Spoonful of Sugar" sequence, Mary helps the kids clean up the trashed nursery by just snapping her fingers. The effect was accomplished by filming a clean nursery, then knocking things over and upending things about to make it look messy, then using the old-school film trick of running the film backwards.

The mechanical robin that sings with Julie Andrews during "Spoonful of Sugar" is credited as being the first audio-animatronic, a form of robotics animation created by Disney Imagineers. Andrews wore a ring to support the robin which connected to a wire that ran down her sleeve and to the floor where there were yards of wiring necessary to perform movements, from flipping a tail to opening a beak to turning a head. The wires were darkened with shoe polish to reduce the risk of reflection from the studio lights. (The technology was later used for shows and attractions at Disney theme parks).

Right at the very heart of the movie, the song "Feed the Birds" recurs throughout the film, but is featured most prominently when Mary sings to the Banks children about the Bird Woman sitting on the Cathedral steps selling crumbs for "tuppence" a bag.

The song has religious overtones and is played in a reverent tempo, similar to a hymn. "Feed the Birds" was the first song written for the film by the Sherman brothers. It is reputed to have been Walt Disney's favorite song – not just his favorite song from the film – his favorite song ever.

The sequence is easily the biggest tearjerker in Disney history.

St. Paul's Cathedral is one of the most famous and most recognizable sights of London, with its dome, framed by the spires of Wren's City churches, dominating the skyline for 300 years. At 365 feet high, it was the tallest building in London from 1710 to 1962, and its dome is also among the highest in the world.

Today, the cathedral's association with *Mary Poppins* remains as strong as ever. Although visitors are asked to refrain from feeding the pigeons on the steps, many come to have their photos taken in the same spot as the Bird Woman. A souvenir "Feed the Birds" cup and saucer is sold in the gift shop.

When Disney archivist Dave Smith went on a search for the "Feed the Birds" snowglobe, whose "snowflakes" are in the shape of the many birds flying around Saint Paul's Cathedral, he finally found it on a shelf in a janitor's office. The janitor explained that he rescued the water-filled globe from a trash can.

Nicknamed "the Ghostest with the Mostess," she was the most famous singing-voice-without-a-face in the history of motion pictures. Among Marni Nixon's unseen roles were the singing voices for Deborah Kerr in *The King and I*, Natalie Wood in *West Side Story*, and Audrey Hepburn in *My Fair Lady*. Nixon lent her voice to four Disney movies, but was only credited in one. She was the ghost soloist in the opening of *Cinderella*, the singing flowers in *Alice in Wonderland*, the voice of cockney geese in the "Jolly Holliday" sequence in *Mary Poppins*. (Her only credited role was the singing voice of Grandmother Fa in Mulan.

Several of the Sherman brothers' songs were deleted from the final print, including "The Chimpanzoo," "Practically Perfect," and "Measure Up," which Mary Poppins was going to sing while measuring the kids with her magical tape measure. A song about Admiral Boom was written for the film, and although the song does not appear in the film, its music can be heard in the score.

A sequence known as "The Magic Compass," consisting of four songs, was dropped from the film in preproduction. One of those songs, "The Beautiful Briny," resurfaced in *Bedknobs and Broomsticks* in 1971.

Among the things that Pamela Travers disliked was the Sherman brothers' score. She wanted the music in the movie to be period pieces such as "Ta Ra Ra Boom De Ay" and "Greensleeves."

During the first year after its release, the *Mary Poppins* soundtrack album sold more than two million copies, spending 14 weeks at Number One on the Billboard charts in 1965, outselling albums released that same year by the Beatles, Elvis Presley and the Rolling Stones. The second cast album sold almost a million, and the "Storyteller" version (narrated by Dal McKennon as Bert) sold nearly a half million.

The Sherman brothers went on to write more motion-picture musical song scores than any other songwriting team in film history. They also composed several top selling pop songs including "You're Sixteen," recorded by rockabilly singer Johnny Burnette whose version peaked at number eight on the Billboard Hot 100 in December 1960 (the song was covered by Ringo Starr in 1973). The original version is featured prominently in the film *American Graffiti.*

Other top-ten hits by the Sherman brothers include "Pineapple Princess," made popular by Annette Funicello in the summer of 1960, and "Let's Get Together," sung by teen actress Hayley Mills in the 1961 Disney film *The Parent Trap* as a duet with herself in her roles as twin sisters.

"He looks like a very old baby," Noël Coward once observed. David Tomlinson was a British character actor, especially in what he once described as "my dim-witted upper-class twit performances." After consideration of performers including David Niven, Terry-Thomas, James Mason, Richard Harris, and George Sanders, Tomlinson was selected for the character of Mr. Banks, even though he had never previously sung professionally. Tomlinson also provided the voice of the parrot head handle on Mary Poppins' umbrella and several of the animated characters in the "Jolly Holiday" sequence, including a penguin waiter and the jockey who allows Mary to pass him in the race. He continued work with Disney after *Mary Poppins*, playing the dastardly villain in *The Love Bug* (1968) and the master wizard Emelius Browne in *Bedknobs and Broomsticks* (1971).

British stage and film actress Glynis Johns is best known for creating the role of Desiree Armfeldt in *A Little Night Music* on Broadway. When Walt Disney first contacted her about the film project, she thought she would be asked to play Mary Poppins. She only agreed to play Mrs. Banks (mother of Jane and Michael and a member of the suffragette movement) if her character had a song written specifically for her. Disney instructed the Sherman brothers to give her a number, so they repurposed a song called "Practically Perfect" and came up with "Sister Suffragette."

Mrs. Banks' first name was originally Cynthia. It was changed to the "more British-sounding" Winifred at Pamela Travers' request.

The Sherman Brothers came up with the idea of Mrs. Banks being involved in the suffragette cause to explain why she should be so neglectful of her children. Their lyrics in "Sister Suffragette" mention Emmeline Pankhurst, leader of the suffragette movement.

Early 20th Century England was a time of strife for women unable to vote in any elections. Suffragettes played an instrumental role in eventually obtaining voting rights for women. This movement preceded the movement in America which occurred several years later.

Often called England's pre-eminent character actress, Hermione Baddeley was nominated for a best-supporting actress Oscar for her work in the 1959 film *Room at the Top*, then demonstrated her versatility in *Mary Poppins* by playing Ellen, the maid of the Banks residence. She was best known to American audiences for her role as the maid, Mrs. Naugatuck, in the television series *Maude*. (Her sister, Angela Baddeley, played Mrs. Bridges, the cook, in the 1970s British television series *Upstairs, Downstairs*).

She was the daughter of a New England orchestra leader, and while she never achieved stardom as a leading lady, the hefty Reta Shaw earned her place as a solid supporting player in such films as *Picnic, The Pajama Game, Pollyanna, That Funny Feeling, Marriage on the Rocks, The Loved One*, and *Bachelor in Paradise*. In *Mary Poppins* she plays Mrs. Brill, the cook of the Banks residence. In the "Step In Time" sequence, she sees too many chimney sweepers and screams, "They're at it again!"

He was known as "Hollywood's favorite butler." Entering films in 1933, Arthur Treacher quickly established himself in butler or servant roles, most notably as "Jeeves" in several Shirley Temple films. After several years away from Hollywood, Treacher returned to portray Constable Jones in *Mary Poppins*, which turned out to be his final film. During the mid-1960s he served as Merv Griffin's TV talk show announcer and sidekick. He lent his name and served as a spokesman for Arthur Treacher's Fish and Chips, a fast-food seafood restaurant chain, underscoring the British character of its food.

Katie Nanna, the nanny who leaves the Banks family at the beginning of the movie, making way for Mary Poppins, is played by Elsa Lanchester. Horror movie buffs recognize her from 1935's *Bride of Frankenstein*, the first sequel to *Frankenstein*, in which she appears both as a subdued Mary Shelley and the Monster's mate, sporting a conical hairdo with white lightning-trace streaks on each side. An English character actress with a long career in theatre, film and television, Lanchester was married to stage and film actor and director Charles Laughton.

Character actress Marjorie Eaton played the role of Miss Persimmon, seen in the park where, after a long pause when the wind blows, her only word was a questioning "yes?" In addition to her roles in film and television, usually cast as domestics, Eaton was an accomplished artist whose work was influenced by Diego Rivera and Frida Kahlo.

Among other "old women" in the park, Mrs. Cory was portrayed by Alma Lawton, who later appeared in *My Fair Lady*. Miss Lark, who owns the dog named Andrew, is played by Marjorie Bennett, a former bathing beauty who acted in a few silent films, then re-emerged after a break of nearly three decades in character parts, usually as gruff housekeepers or snooty socialites.

Mary Poppins was the second of three Disney films that Matthew Garber (Michael Banks) and Karen Dotrice (Jane Banks) appeared in, both aged seven. Their first film together was *The Three Lives of Thomasina* (1963), and their third was *The Gnome-Mobile* (1967).

The daughter of two Shakespearean actors, Kay and Roy Dotrice, Karen's godfather was actor Charles Laughton, who was married to Elsa Lanchester, one of the supporting cast members in *Mary Poppins*. Karen later played a housemaid in the 1970s British TV series, *Upstairs Downstairs*.

While in India in 1976, Matthew contracted hepatitis. By the time his family could get him home, it had spread to his pancreas and was untreatable. He never recovered and died at age twenty-one.

Director Robert Stevenson didn't inform the two child actors about "surprises," so their on-screen reactions would be genuine. The kids couldn't see what was being fed to Mary's carpet bag from under the table, so when she pulled hat stands and potted plants out of her bag, they were stunned. They were not told that it was Dick Van Dyke in makeup as old Mr. Dawes, and they were genuinely afraid of the "horrible old man."

Matthew Garber, who plays young Michael, was afraid of heights, which meant filming the tea party on the ceiling scene was a big challenge for him. He was bribed with 10 cents for every take during the suspended "I Love to Laugh" sequence.

Plastic casts of Matthew and Karen's bottoms were made on the first day of shooting for the seats they would use on to go up the bannister with Mary.

Larri Thomas began her career in a string of television commercials. After appearing in minor roles in *Peter Gunn* and *The Lucy-Desi Comedy Hour*, she became one of the six Goldwyn Girls, picked by Samuel Goldwyn to go on tour for the movie, *Guys and Dolls*. She served as a stand-in for Julie Andrews in *Mary Poppins* (and later in *The Sound of Music*). Uncredited for a brief on-screen appearance in *Mary Poppins*, she is the woman in the carriage who blows a kiss to Bert during "Chim Chim Cheree."

He played Watson in the 1932 film *Sherlock Holmes*, then Holmes himself a year later in *A Study in Scarlet*. Reginald Owen was cast as Ebenezer Scrooge in the 1938 film version of Charles Dickens' *A Christmas Carol*. Although Stanley Holloway was Disney's first choice for the role, Owen was amusing and bombastic as Admiral Boom, the cannon-happy eccentric neighbor in *Mary Poppins*. (In August 1964, Owen's Bel-Air mansion was rented out to the Beatles, who were performing at the Hollywood Bowl).

Don Barclay had supplied his voice to several Disney animated features when he was cast at Mr. Binnacle, Admiral Boom's first mate. Barclay, whose many roles stretched all the way back to Keystone Cops comedies in the silent era, was also known as a cartoonist and painter. His painting of a tiny skier jumping off Bob Hope's nose can be seen at the Library of Congress.

It was Walt Disney himself who came up with the idea that when Admiral Boom fires his cannon, everything in the Banks' house shakes and topples, with women in the house running around to right everything that is repeatedly set askew. As Walt walked around the set he said, "How about having the vase fall off and the maid catches it with her toe?" Or, "Let's have the grand piano roll across the room and the mother catches it as she straightens the picture frame."

The older brother of Barbara Stanwyck (whose real name was Ruby Stevens), Bert Stevens appeared in nearly 250 films without a single on-screen credit. He had walk-on roles in such films as *Citizen Kane, Meet John Doe, I Married a Witch, Adam's Rib, Titanic, The Caine Mutiny, An Affair to Remember, Some Like It Hot, North by Northwest, The Manchurian Candidate*, and *Marnie*, before being cast as the top-hatted man in the bank in *Mary Poppins*.

He was a member of a family who performed in the music halls of Scotland and Northern Ireland during the 1930s and 40s. Jimmy Logan went on to appear in two films in the *Carry On* series, based on the British comic tradition of the music hall. In *Mary Poppins* he is the doorman who chases after the children in the bank.

Other veteran character actors who appear in the bank scene include Doris Lloyd, Cyril Delevanti, Frank Baker, Clive Halliday, Arthur Malet, and King Mojave.

Betty Lou Gerson first worked for Disney in 1950, when she provided the "Once upon a time…" narration for the animated classic *Cinderella*. In *Mary Poppins* she plays the Old Crone who promises to hide the Banks children after they run away from the bank. In her most notable work, she was the voice of Cruella De Vil in the Disney animated feature *101 Dalmations*.

George DeNormand, soldier of fortune, middleweight prizefighter, and one of the founding fathers of modern movie stunt work, performed stunts and played bit roles in scores of action thrillers, B-Westerns, and serials, working mostly for Republic Pictures. After his own hair went white, he became the established stunt double for Spencer Tracy. DeNormand is the white-haired man seen walking briskly through the park.

Best-known for his role as the voice of Gumby in Art Clokey's stop-motion clay animation TV series, *The Gumby Show*, character actor and voice artist Dallas McKennon performed many character voices for Disney. His distinctive voice can be heard in films such as *Lady and the Tramp*, *Sleeping Beauty*, *101 Dalmatians*, and *Bedknobs and Broomsticks*. In *Mary Poppins*, he provides the voice of the Merry-Go-Round guard.

Alan Napier, who portrayed Alfred Pennyworth, Bruce Wayne's faithful butler on the 1960s-era *Batman* TV series lends his voice to a huntsman, a hound, and a reporter. Napier was the cousin of British Prime Minister Neville Chamberlain, and his wife, Aileen Dickens Bouchier Hawksley, was a great-granddaughter of Charles Dickens.

A voice actress who appeared in dozens of Disney cartoons and animated films, Ginny Tyler sang for several barnyard animals in the "Jolly Holiday" sequence.

Robert Stevenson first established himself as a director in Great Britain, where his works included an adaptation of H. Rider Haggard's *King Solomon's Mines*. He moved to Hollywood at about the same time as Alfred Hitchcock but with far less success until he joined Walt Disney's Buena Vista division. There he would go on to make 19 films, including *Kidnapped*, *The Absent-Minded Professor*, *In Search of the Castaways*, *The Misadventures of Merlin Jones*, *The Monkey's Uncle*, *That Darn Cat*, and *The Love Bug*. Stevenson was the obvious choice to direct *Mary Poppins* – he had been a boy with an English nanny in an upper-middle-class family in Edwardian England. The film was his masterpiece.

In 1971, Stevenson made *Bedknobs and Broomsticks*, a musical that tried unsuccessfully to recapture the *Mary Poppins* magic.

Hamilton "Ham" Luske was chosen by Walt Disney to be the first animator put on the production of *Snow White and the Seven Dwarfs* (1937), the first full-length cel animated feature in American motion picture history, and tasked with the challenge of making Snow White more believably human and realistic than any of the Disney studio's previous animated characters. He supervised the animation of Snow White herself, a character generations of audiences fell in love with. Luske directed the "Jolly Holiday" animation in *Mary Poppins*. For his effort, he won the Academy Award for Best Special Visual Effects.

Set director Emile Kuri, an eight-time Oscar nominee and winner of two Academy Awards, was born in Cuernavaca, Mexico, to Lebanese parents who eventually moved to Los Angeles. Kuri worked with some of the biggest names in Hollywood and on some of the most memorable films in history. He designed the Main Street setting of Jimmy Stewart's hometown for Frank Capra's *It's a Wonderful Life*. In 1952, he joined the Disney Studio where he remained for twenty three years. Prior to the filming of *Mary Poppins*, Disney had Kuri redecorate the home he had rented for Julie Andrews with English antiques, and after filming was over, Andrews had Kuri design the interiors for her home in England.

Working with Walt Disney in the early days of animation, Ub Iwerks was responsible for creating the character of Mickey Mouse in 1922. He left to form his own animation company in 1930, then returned to Disney in 1940 where he made enormous advances in the field of optical printing and matte photography, seamlessly combining animation with live action. For *Mary Poppins*, Van Dyke and Andrews were photographed in front of a colored backdrop; special film was used that was sensitive only to the narrow band of spectrum used in the color backing. When processed, this film rendered the backdrop color as opaque and other foreground subjects as transparent. The roll of film served as the matte to composite "Mary" and "Bert" into the Disney artwork so they could dance with animated penguins. The layered composing of live actors with the cartoons was made possible by the development of a color-based traveling matte system invented by Iwerks, along with Wadswortyh E. Pohl and Petros Vlahos.

The blend of live action and animation did not begin with *Mary Poppins*. A young Walt Disney combined live action and animation in the mid-1920s with the *Alice* comedies, a series of films in which a live action little girl named Alice (played by Virginia Davis) and an animated cat named Julius have adventures in an animated landscape.

Animator and imagineer Blaine Gibson designed the carousel horses in *Mary Poppins*, with the faces of each sculpted as caricatures of their riders. (Note the prominent chin on Dick Van Dyke's horse). The horses move up and down using a technique called "mechanical manual tube suspension." (Gibson also created the iconic sculpture of Walt Disney holding hands with Mickey Mouse installed at Disneyland's Central Hub).

A noted painter of fine art in his own right, William Samuel Cook "Peter" Ellenshaw became famous for the hand-painted mattes he created for Disney films, including over one hundred matte paintings done on glass to recreate the London skyline of 1910 in *Mary Poppins*.

Special effects for the film were provided by Ellenshaw, Eustace Lycett and Robert A. Mattey (who went on to create the mechanical shark used in *Jaws*). Flying sequences were handled by second unit director Arthur J. Vitarelli, who had previously staged the flying basketball and football sequences in *The Absent-Minded Professor* and *Son of Flubber*.

She was the hairstylist who created the wacky, exploding hairdo that comedienne Phyllis Diller was known for. La Rue Matheron worked in the Disney make-up department for approximately 50 films during a twenty-year span. The softly-swept updo of Mary Poppins (a wig worn by Julie Andrews) was styled by Matheron according to specific instructions by Walt Disney.

The opening shot of Mary Poppins sitting on a cloud includes a gag originally used in Disney's *Dumbo*. While Mary checks her make-up, her carpetbag slides "through" the cloud. She catches it repeatedly just before it falls to oblivion. The stork delivering Dumbo does the same thing with his bundle.

Notice Mary's stance, with heels together and toes pointed outwards in a balletic position. The inspiration lies in Pamela Travers' background. Long before she was a writer, Travers was a dancer and actor, performing in pantomimes in Sydney and later dancing as an interlude within Shakespeare productions.

Julie Andrews as Mary Poppins quotes the opening line of *Endymion*, an 1818 poem by John Keats, when she "A thing of beauty is a joy forever," as she pulls a potted plant out of her carpet bag. The same quote is used by Gene Wilder in *Willy Wonka and the Chocolate Factory* (1971).

Filming of *Mary Poppins* began in late August of 1963. Production required the use of all four soundstages on the Disney studio lot. It was decided that every frame of film would be shot indoors, conjuring up a consistently stylized, confectioner's imagining of London. The film utilized the talents of every artist, craftsman, and technician on the Disney payroll.

The 18 cherry trees on Cherry Tree Lane were real – but the blooms were not. To create the effect of blossom-laden branches, artists hand-mounted thousands of twigs and paper cherry blossoms. The houses on Cherry Tree Lane were built on a diminishing scale, getting smaller as the lane progressed.

Walt Disney had purchased the rights to the Travers' book *Mary Poppins* – but not the rights to the illustrations. As a result, Tony Walton was not allowed to use any details from the book's illustrations in designing costumes or sets for the film. At Walt's suggestion, the time of the story was changed from the 1930s to 1910, since they saw more rich visual and musical opportunities there. That allowed the Disney team to use the styles of late Edwardian England, and Walton would avoid any accusations of copying the original illustrations from the book.

Look closely at the nannies gathered outside the Banks' home on Cherry Tree Lane before the wind blows them away and Mary Poppins arrives. You will recognize that some of them are actually stunt men dressed as old English nannies.

The scene was planned for animation, but in one of the production meetings, Walt asked if the scene could be shot live. Second unit director Arthur Vitarelli set up a large wind machine in the background and had each "woman" connected to two wires and separate counterweights. A man with a winch then pulled them up and away.

Originally, there was an eerie scene in which toys in the nursery magically come alive to torment the children and teach them a lesson. In test screenings the sequence proved frightening for younger children and was removed in the final cut. (However, in the Broadway musical of *Mary Poppins*, the toys coming alive idea is used).

Another sequence that didn't make the final cut was a trip around the world guided by a magic compass. The children would spin the compass and end up in another land. Walt thought it was too extraneous to the plot, so it was dropped.

Mary's ever-present umbrella with a parrot-head handle doesn't reveal that it can speak until the end of the film. When it does speak, the voice is none other than David Tomlinson (who plays Mr. Banks).

During the 1800s, parrots were introduced to England as household pets. Middle-class families found them to be intelligent, charismatic, colorful, and musical.

The filming of *Mary Poppins* wound up with the final flying scenes. According to Julie Andrews, "They saved all the really dangerous stuff until the end of the film, just in case I had a horrible accident and they lost me." In fact, on the very last day of shooting, with Julie high up on the grid and wearing a flying harness, a support wire gave way and she dropped about a foot. After calling to the technician to lower her slowly, she fell to the stage like a "ton of bricks."

On the evening of August 27, 1964, *Mary Poppins* was launched at Graumann's Chinese Theatre on Hollywood Boulevard, the same day that the Democratic National Convention in Atlantic City ended, having nominated incumbent President Lyndon Johnson for a full term and Hubert Humphrey as his running mate. (Prior to the 1964 premiere of *Mary Poppins*, Walt Disney had not attended a studio premiere since *Snow White and the Seven Dwarfs* in 1937).

The Disney staff did not invite Pamela Travers to the premiere, so she undertook to invite herself and flew out the day before with the financial support of her publisher. She reportedly hated the film so much that she became visibly upset and wept during the screening, to the embarrassment of Disney and his staff, and, confronting Walt at the after-party, she insisted, "All the animation has to go." Walt replied, "Pamela, that ship has sailed."

A constant thorn in Disney's side, Travers was upset by billboards and publicity that called the film Walt Disney's *Mary Poppins*. She thought it should have read P. L. Travers' *Mary Poppins*, Screened by Disney. In a letter to her London publisher, she complained that the film was "Disney through and through, spectacular, colourful, gorgeous but all wrapped around mediocrity of thought, poor glimmerings of understanding and oversimplification."

Travers hated the animated sequence. She hated the house the Banks family lived in. She hated that they changed the time period. She hated that Mary Poppins was pretty. She hated the songs. And she loathed Dick Van Dyke. Yet despite all her displeasure, *Mary Poppins* became a huge annuity for her, and after release of the film, sales of her books tripled.

Movie critics, many of whom had pooh-poohed Disney's post-war films, devoted columns of praise to *Mary Poppins*. Bosley Crowther wrote in *The New York Times*: "the visual and aural felicities (Disney and company) have added to this sparkling film – the enchantments of a beautiful production, some deliciously animated sequences, some exciting and nimble dancing and a spinning musical score – make it the nicest entertainment that has opened at the Music Hall this year." Judith Crist in *The Herald Tribune*: "The performers surpass even the technical wizardry of the film... Miss Andrews is superb at song and dance and the heart of the matter." Hollis Alpert in *Saturday Review*: "One of the most magnificent pieces of entertainment ever to come from Hollywood."

If there's a complaint to be made with a film that is, as Mary Poppins would have it, "practically perfect in every way," it may be a bit too long for some, especially young children. Film critic Nathan Cone has suggested that at nearly 2 hours and 20 minutes, *Mary Poppins* is a lot to take in one dose – even with a spoonful of sugar. In fact, some showings of the film in England were presented with an intermission.

During filming, director Robert Wise asked Walt Disney if he could visit the *Mary Poppins* set and view some of the daily rushes. Walt, keen to show off his new star (Julie Andrews), agreed to show forty minutes of rough-cut footage. Based solely on that visit, Wise offered Andrews the role of Maria Von Trapp in *The Sound of Music,* his motion picture adaptation of the Broadway musical.

Not only one of the highest-grossing films of the year, but *Mary Poppins* was Disney's highest-grossing film up to that time. The film cost the studio $5.2 million to make, and with revenues of an astounding $50 million worldwide in the first year alone, his earnings provided Disney the cash to purchase 27,500 acres in central Florida and finance the development of Walt Disney World.

When the film was shown in Moscow, the government had to convert the Sports Palace into a theater and welcomed eight thousand viewers at each of two screenings.

With five wins (Best Actress – Julie Andrews, Best Song – "Chim Chim Cher-ee," Best Score – Richard and Robert Sherman, Best Visual Effects, and Best Film Editing) out of 13 nominations in total, *Mary Poppins* marked the Disney studio's single most successful night at the Academy Awards. Never before or since has a single Disney film won as many Oscars in one evening.

The film was so successful in its theatrical release that it continued playing throughout 1965, giving it a chance to compete against *The Sound of Music*. *Mary Poppins* was the highest grossing film of 1965 (*The Sound of Music* came in second).

Disney licensed a long list of merchandising tie-ins to the film, among them girls' dresses, dolls, jewelry, and books titled *Walt Disney's Mary Poppins* (After release of the film, Disney books outsold Travers' own Poppins books by 5 to 1). The National Sugar Company jumped on the bandwagon, launching a "Spoonful of Sugar" advertising campaign, while a British company advertised Mary Poppins Nylons.

The original agreement between Travers and Disney included a standard provision for a sequel, yet after his achievement with *Mary Poppins*, Walt refused to entertain suggestions for a sequel, explaining, "I don't want to go back and cover the same ground."

The Sherman brothers and Walt shared a bond until Disney's death in 1966. On Fridays, at the end of his work week, Walt would often invite the brothers to his office and ask them to "play it." The song he wanted to hear was "Feed the Birds" from *Mary Poppins*, his personal favorite. Upon hearing the song, he would always cry.

Mary Poppins was the only film personally produced by Walt Disney to be nominated for a Best Picture Oscar. He regarded the film as one of the crowning achievements of his career, the securing of his reputation as one of Hollywood's most enduring filmmakers.

Mary Poppins was released on video in 1981 and has not been out of print since. It also became the first Disney film to be released on DVD. In 2001, the film was rereleased in a special "sing-along" edition with subtitles added to the musical numbers so audiences could join in with the onscreen vocalists.

In December of 2013, the Library of Congress selected *Mary Poppins* for preservation in the National Film Registry. It is the only live-action Disney film ever selected.

REFERENCES

Travers, P. L. *Mary Poppins from A to Z* (Harcourt Brace & World, 1962).

Thomas, Bob. *Walt Disney: An American Original* (Simon and Schuster, 1976).

Barrier, Michael. *The Animated Man: A Life of Walt Disney* (University of California Press, 2007).

Bergsten, Staffan. *Mary Poppins and Myth* (Almqvist & Wiksell International, 1978).

Carey, Mary. *The Story of Walt Disney's Motion Picture Mary Poppins* (Whitman Publishing, 1964).

Demers, Patricia. *P. L. Travers* (Twayne, 1991).

Gabler, Neal. *Walt Disney: The Triumph of the American Imagination* (Alfred A. Knopf, 2006).

Grilli, Giorgia (translated by Jennifer Varney). *Myth, Symbol, and Meaning in Mary Poppins: The Governess as Provocateur* (Routledge, 2007).

Watts, Steven. *The Magic Kingdom: Walt Disney and the American Way of Life* (Houghton Mifflin, 1997).

Schickel, Richard. *The Disney Version: The Life, Times, Art and Commerce of Walt Disney* (Simon and Schuster, 1968).

Smoodin, Eric, ed. *Disney Discourse: Producing the Magic Kingdom* (Routledge, 1994).

Greene, Katherine and Richard. *The Man Behind the Magic: The Story of Walt Disney* (Viking, 1991).

Kennedy, Matthew. *Roadshow! The Fall of Film Musicals in the 1960s* (Oxford University Press, 2014).

Eliot, Marc. *Walt Disney: Hollywood's Dark Prince* (Carol Publishing, 1993).

Andrews, Julie. *Home: A Memoir of My Early Years* (Hyperion, 2008).

Stirling, Richard. *Julie Andrews: An Intimate Biography* (St. Martin's Press, 2007).

Sayers, Frances Clarke, and Charles M. Weisenberg. 1965. "Walt Disney Accused." *Horn Book Magazine* 40: 602–611.

Flanagan, Caitlin. "Becoming Mary Poppins: P. L. Travers, Walt Disney, and the Making of a Myth." *New Yorker*, December 19, 2005.

In Invitation

With a view to future editions, suggestions
for additions, corrections of errors,
or changes in factual data are invited.

The publishers cordially invite you to submit your
criticisms of this book and any other volumes that
bear the History Company name. Ideas for new
books or reprints to be added to our catalogue
are also most welcome.

Please address your criticisms, corrections,
or suggestions to:
support@historycompany.com